What any author wants is for his books to become dog-eared and familiar. I've been lucky enough that my very young readers are particularly adept at giving their books doggy ears in no time at all.

And of all my books, perhaps it's those about Kipper that get the doggiest ears of all, which I guess is kind of appropriate.

Mick Inkpen

First published in 2001
by Hodder Children's Books

This edition published in 2016

Text and illustrations copyright © Mick Inkpen 2001

Hodder Children's Books
An imprint of
Hachette Children's Group
Part of Hodder & Stoughton
Carmelite House
50 Victoria Embankment
London EC4Y 0DZ

A catalogue record of this book is available
from the British Library.

ISBN: 978 1 444 93048 1
10 9 8 7 6 5 4 3 2 1

Printed in Italy by Printer Trento

An Hachette UK Company
www.hachette.co.uk

Kipper's New Pet

Mick Inkpen

Hodder
Children's
Books

Pig was writing the invitations to his birthday party.
This was his present list.

    1. A pet. Like a rabbit, or a guinea pig, or something.

    2. A little mouse or a gerbil.

    3. Anything else.

        (But mostly I would like Number 1, or Number 2.)

He put the names on the envelopes and wondered what kind of pet he would get.

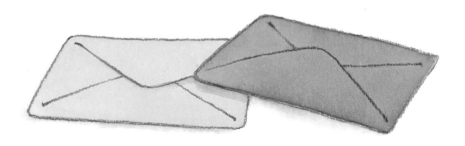

When Kipper's invitation arrived, he read it and rushed off to the pet shop to choose a pet for Pig.

The rabbit? Too sleepy.

The guinea pigs? Too timid.

The mouse? Too shy.

The stick insect?
　　Too much like a stick.
　　Boring.

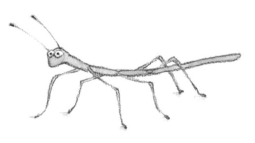

ut the hamster? The hamster was not sleepy, nor timid, nor shy, and it wasn't like a stick at all!

It was perfect.

'One of these please!' said Kipper.

At home Kipper gave the hamster some sunflower seeds. It stuffed them into its cheeks.

'Are you always this hungry?' said Kipper. The hamster ran up Kipper's arm and sat on his shoulder, cleaning its whiskers. Then it ran down the other arm and rolled across the table.

'You can do a roly poly!' said Kipper. 'You're so clever!' The hamster did it again.

The morning of the party, Roly Poly woke Kipper by nibbling on his ear.

'I wish I didn't have to give you to Pig today,' said Kipper.

At breakfast Kipper began to think that maybe he would keep Roly and buy a rabbit for Pig instead.

'No. He'd like you better,' sighed Kipper. 'Come on. Let's wrap up your cage.'

Kipper got out some scissors and some sticky tape, and unrolled a roll of wrapping paper.

Roly ran into the cardboard tube and popped out at the other end, making Kipper giggle.

Then he slid all the way down the tube and rolled across the floor, making Kipper giggle again.

It gave Kipper an idea...

...a big idea.

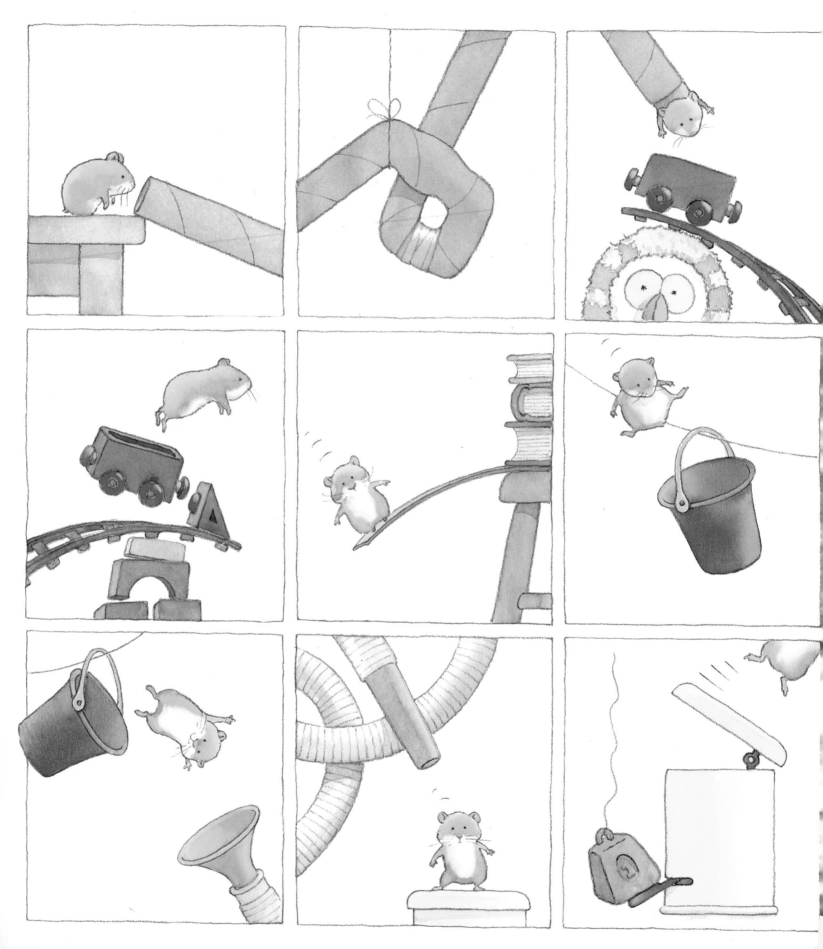

This was Kipper's big idea. It took him ages. But it worked perfectly! 'You're the best birthday present ever!' said Kipper.

It was then that he remembered...

...Pig's party!

Kipper rushed off to Pig's house. Halfway there he met Jake and Tiger, coming the other way.

'Where were you?' said Tiger. 'The party's over!' But Kipper wasn't listening. He was thinking about Roly Poly.

'I can't stop!' he said. 'I don't think he likes it in there very much.'

Jake and Tiger began to giggle.

'Oh, no! Not another one!' said Tiger.

'I'm sorry I'm late!' said Kipper
to Pig, as he opened the door.
'I was playing with
your present!
He's brilliant,
isn't he?'

Then he noticed that Pig was
holding a rabbit, a mouse and two
guinea pigs, and there was a
stick insect crawling across his head.
'What are those?' said Kipper.
'They're my presents,' said Pig.

They sat down at Pig's table and Kipper fed Roly with pieces of left-over party cake.

'So he's not really what you wanted?' said Kipper.

'He's exactly what I wanted,' said Pig, 'before I had all these.'

He pointed at his other pets. 'But it's my own fault. I should have thought of something else to put on my present list.'

Kipper took a big bite of cake
for himself.

'He's very nice though, isn't he?'
said Kipper. 'His name is Roly Poly.
Because he can do roly polies.
He's really good at them!
And he's always hungry. He keeps
his food in his cheeks! Look!'

Pig looked at Roly's little,
fat face. It was his
turn to have
an idea.

'Kipper?' said Pig. 'Would you do me a favour? Would you look after him for me?'

Kipper was so surprised he almost choked on his cake.

'What! Take him home, you mean?' said Kipper.

Pig nodded.

'So, he'd still be yours, but I'd look after him?'

Pig nodded again.

'Oh, yes!'

said Kipper.

He said it so loudly, that all of Pig's pets jumped off the table and hid underneath.

Kipper picked up Roly Poly, sat him back down and fed him another piece of cake. Roly Poly stopped eating for a second, hiccuped...

...and started eating again.

'My children absolutely LOVE all of Mick Inkpen's books, and I still love reading Kipper to them, even when it's for the hundredth time. . .'

CRESSIDA COWELL

'Storytelling at its best.' DAVID MELLING

Mick Inkpen

Billy's
Beetle
Mick Inkpen

The
Blue Balloon
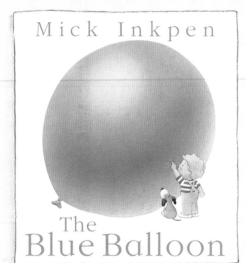

Nothing

MICK INKPEN
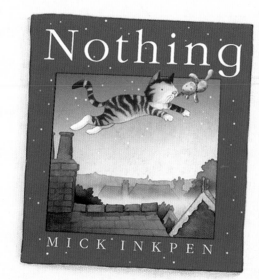

One Bear
at Bedtime
Mick Inkpen
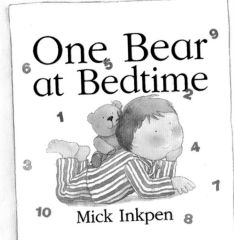

We are
wearing out
the
naughty
step
Mick Inkpen

Threadbear
MICK INKPEN
WITH FOLD-OUT PAGES